Marine Animals
Stained Glass Pattern Book

Carolyn Relei

DOVER PUBLICATIONS, INC., *New York*

Published in Canada by General Publishing Company, Ltd., 30 Lesmill
Road, Don Mills, Toronto, Ontario.

Marine Animals Stained Glass Pattern Book is a new work, first published by
Dover Publications, Inc., in 1992.

DOVER *Pictorial Archive* SERIES

Manufactured in the United States of America
Dover Publications, Inc., 31 East 2nd Street, Mineola, N.Y. 11501

Library of Congress Cataloging-in-Publication Data

Relei, Carolyn.
    Marine animals stained glass pattern book / Carolyn Relei.
        p.   cm. —(Dover pictorial archive series)
    ISBN 0-486-27016-5 (pbk.)
    1. Glass craft—Patterns.   2. Glass staining and painting—Pat-
terns. I. Title. II. Series.
TT298.R46 1992
748.5'022'2—dc20   91-34469
                                                                  CIP

Publisher's Note

The shimmering lights, shifting colors and fascinating animals seen in an underwater setting offer constant pleasure to swimmers, divers and aquarists everywhere. For transferring these subtle effects and dazzling creatures to your own home in an artifact of lasting value, what more appropriate medium than stained glass?

This collection of 82 patterns by stained-glass artist Carolyn Relei encompasses lovely underwater panoramas as well as serene seashore settings, some relatively realistic, a few somewhat more abstract. The patterns feature a broad variety of marine animals, both vertebrate and invertebrate, including fish, whales, snails, sea anemones, walruses, sea birds and starfish, all in a diversity of surroundings to enable you to express a whole spectrum of marine moods in stained glass to enhance any setting.

The designs may be enlarged or reduced to suit your needs. They are readily adaptable for use in windows, door panels, lightcatchers, mirrors, boxes, candle shelters, panels, mobiles, lampshades and other crafts applications. This book is intended to be used in conjunction with a suitable stained-glass instruction book (such as *Stained Glass Craft* by J. A. F. Divine and G. Blachford, Dover Publications, Inc., 0-486-22812-6). All materials needed, including general instructions and tools for beginners, can usually be purchased from local craft and hobby stores listed in your Yellow Pages.

Clownfish

Sea Anemone

Underwater Scene

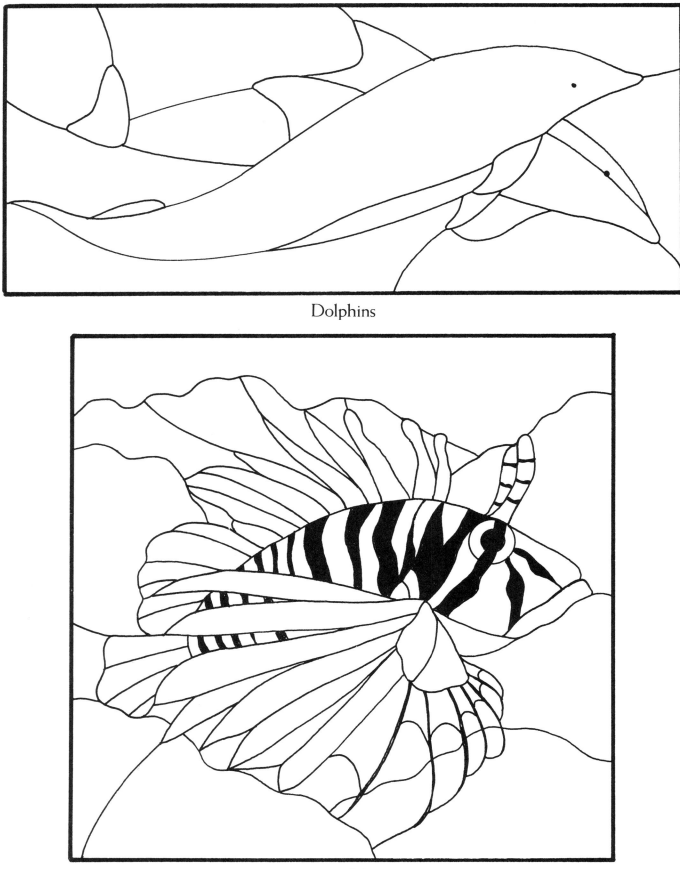

Dolphins

Lionfish

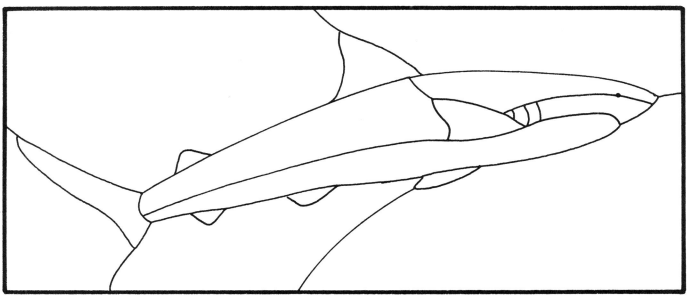

Shark

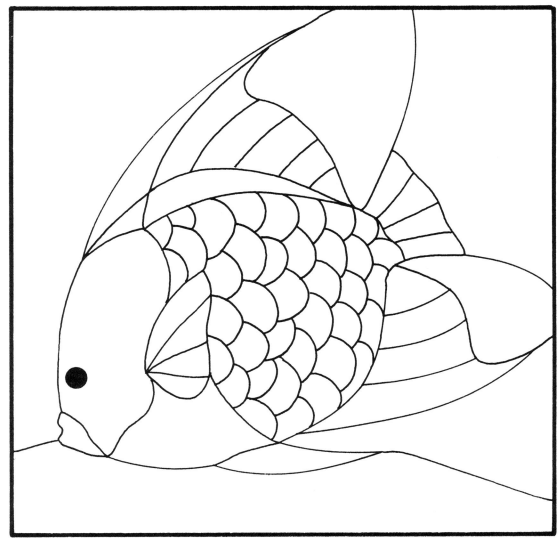

Angelfish

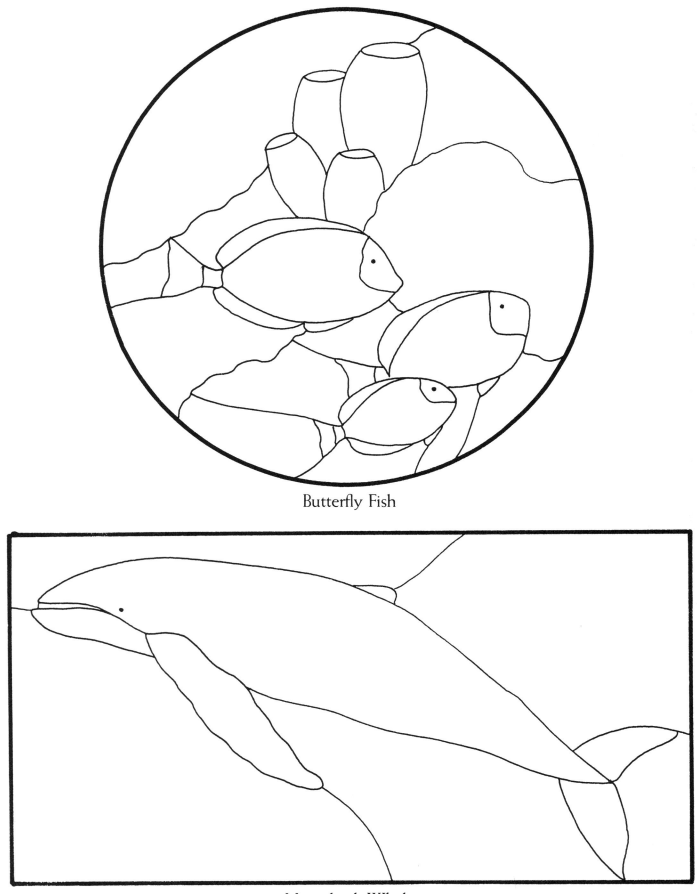

Butterfly Fish

Humpback Whale

Underwater Scene

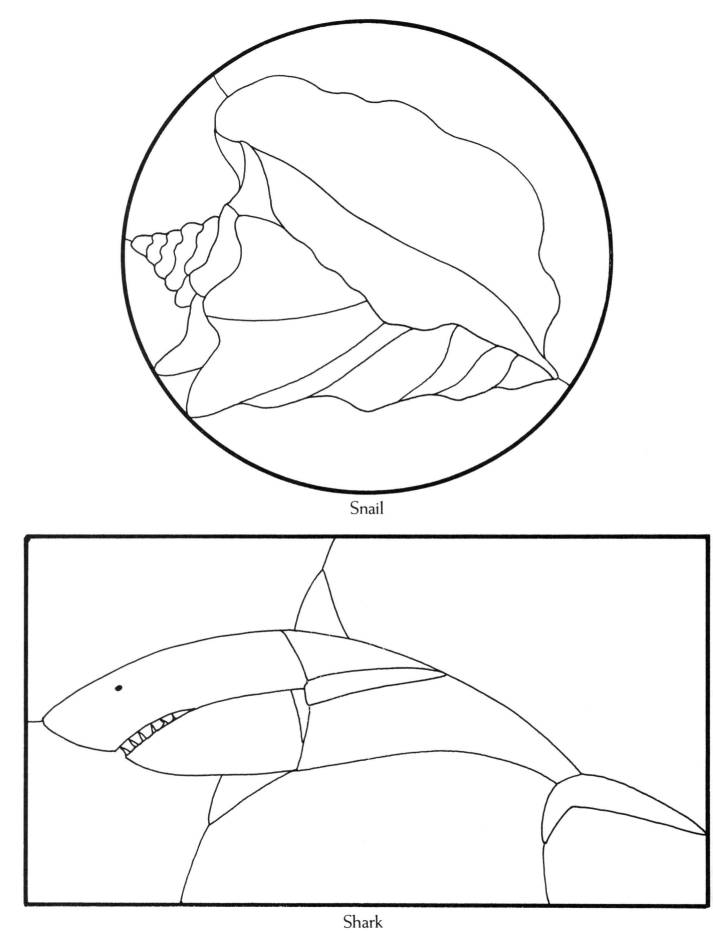

Snail

Shark

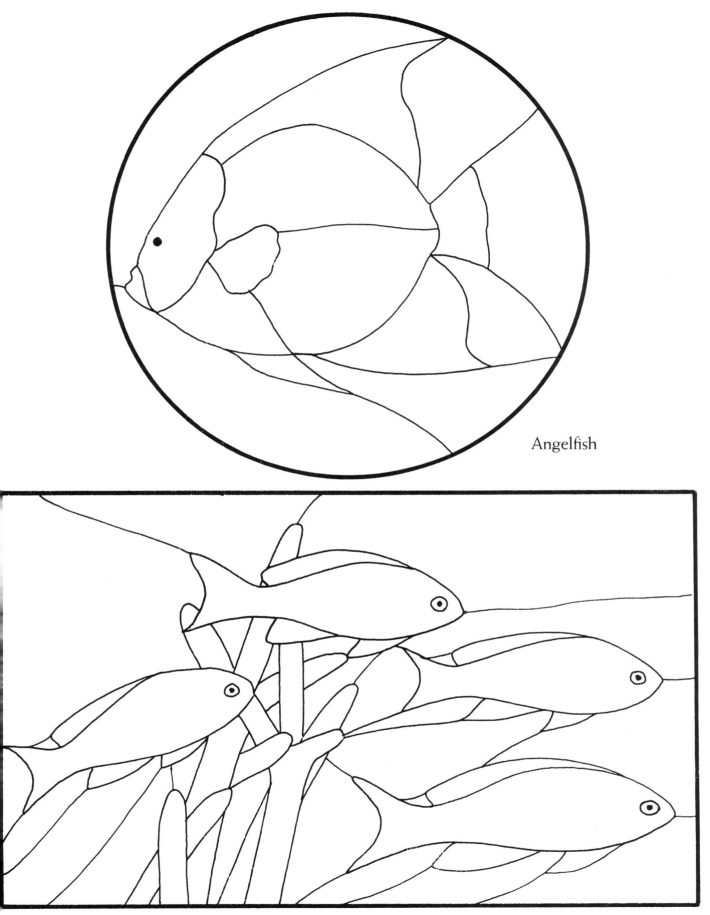

Angelfish

Surfperches

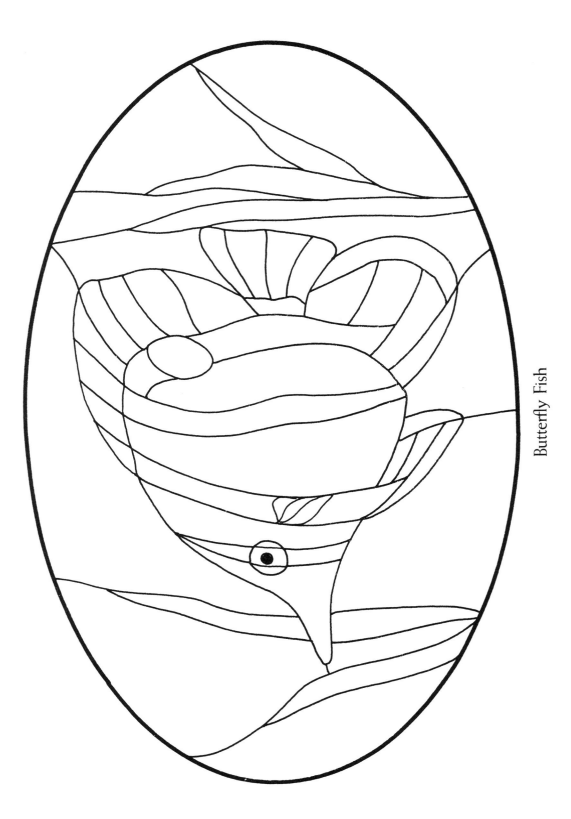

Butterfly Fish

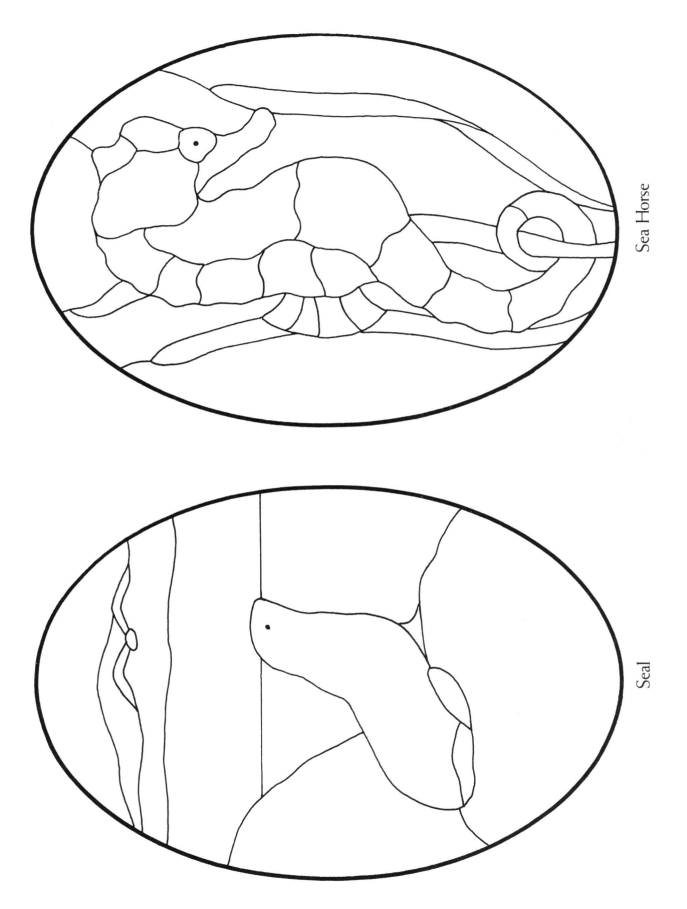

Sea Horse

Seal

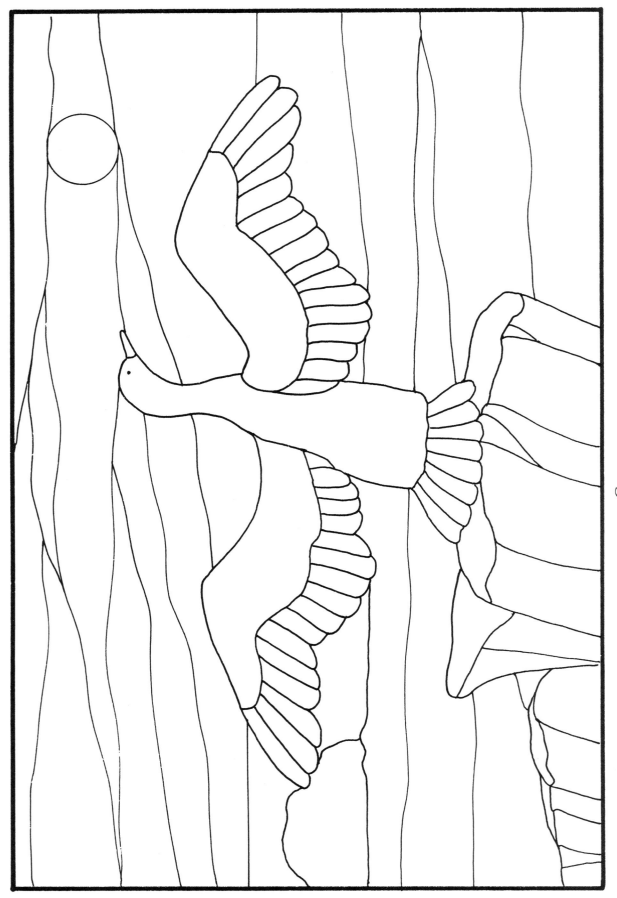

Cormorant

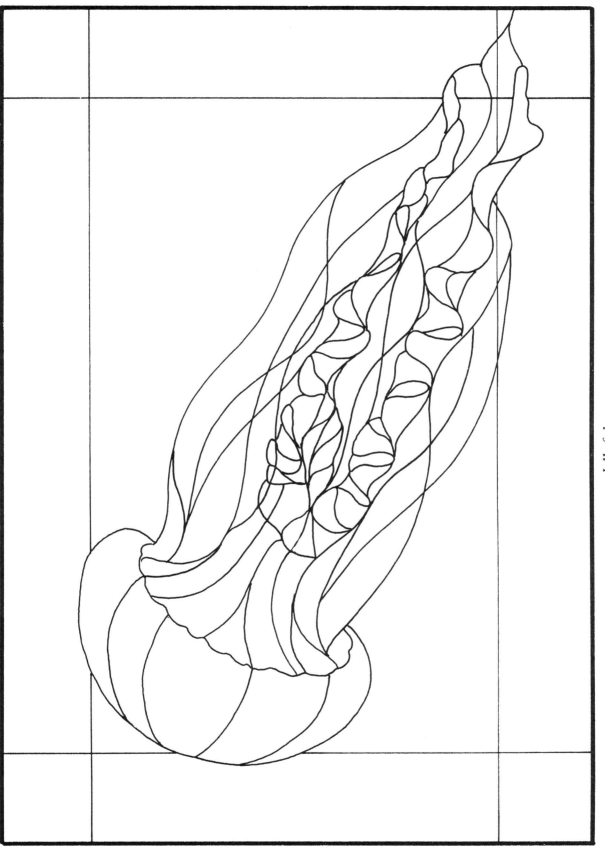

Jellyfish

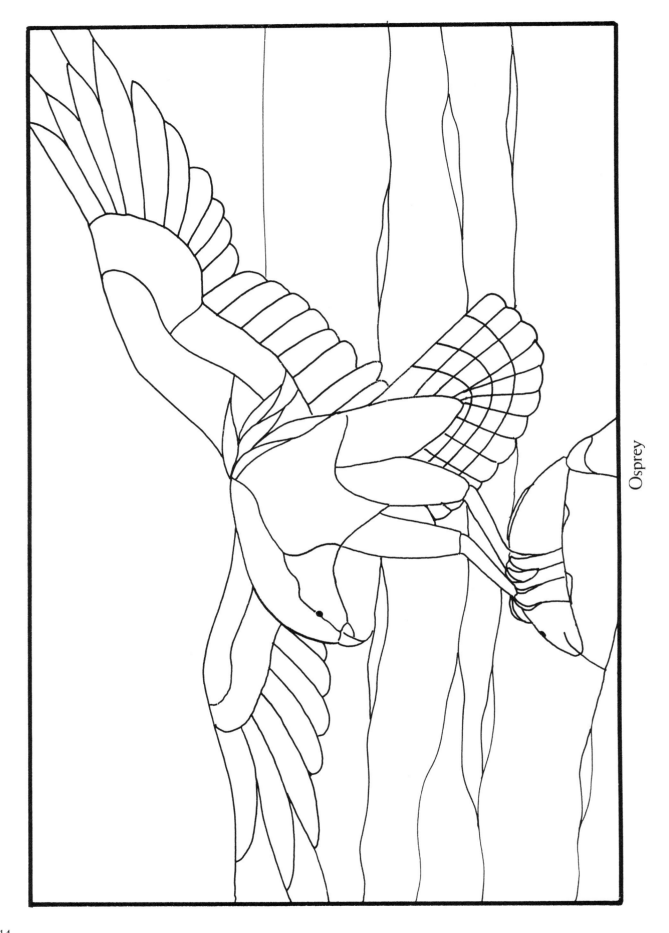

Osprey

14

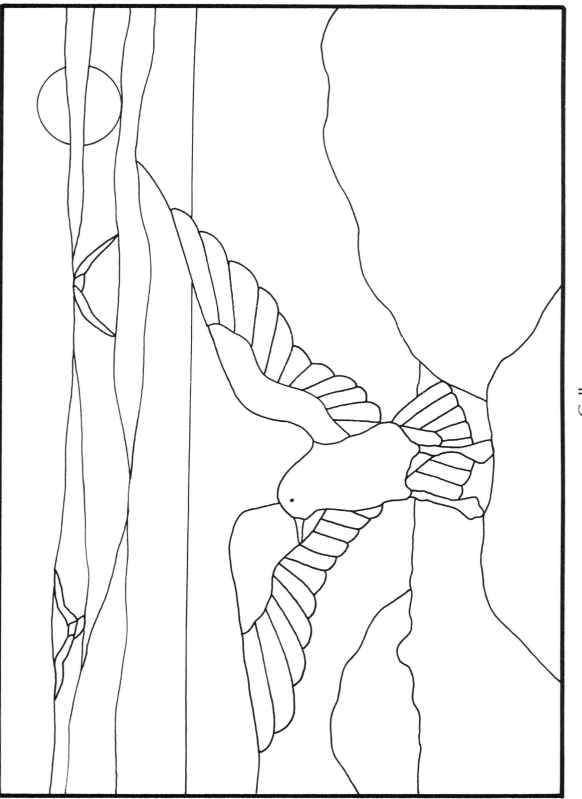

Gulls

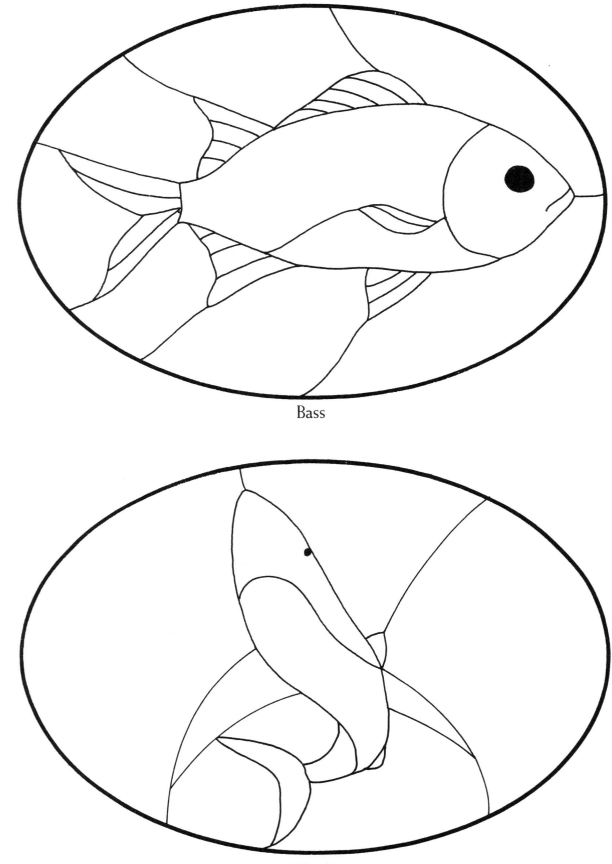

Bass

Shark

Pelicans

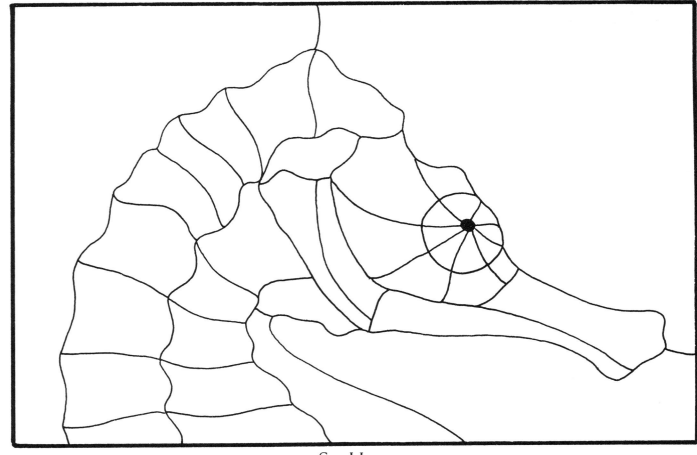

Sea Horse

Butterfly Fish

Gull

Sunfish

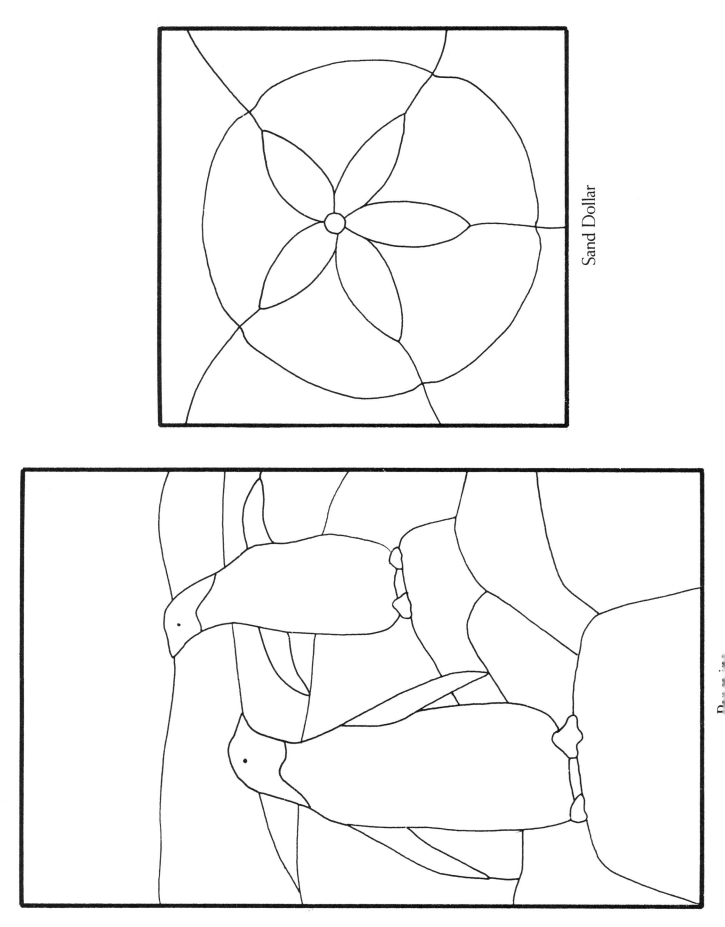

Sand Dollar

Penguins

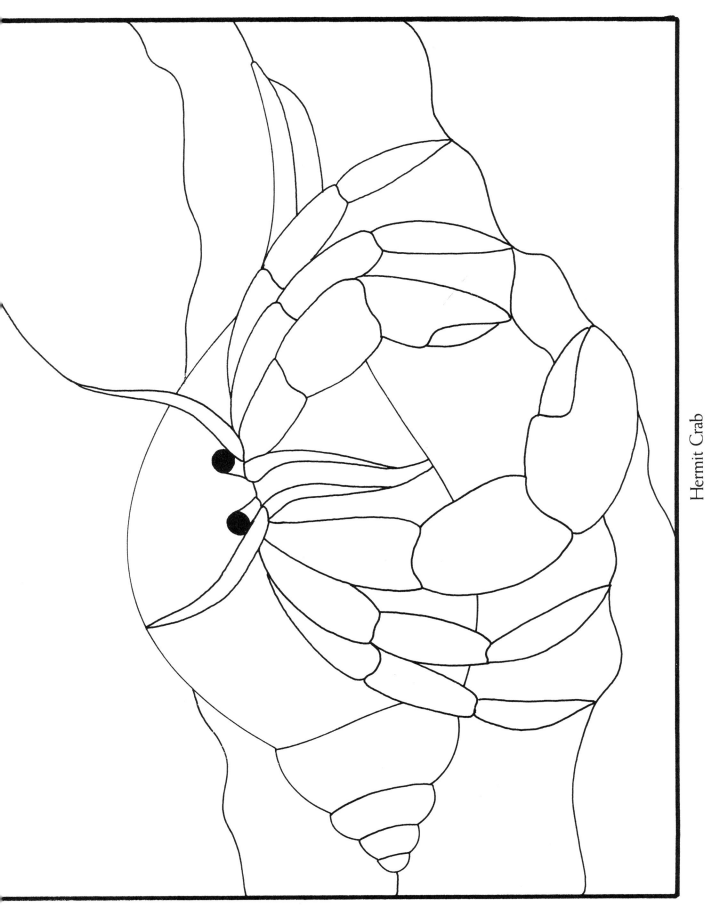

Hermit Crab

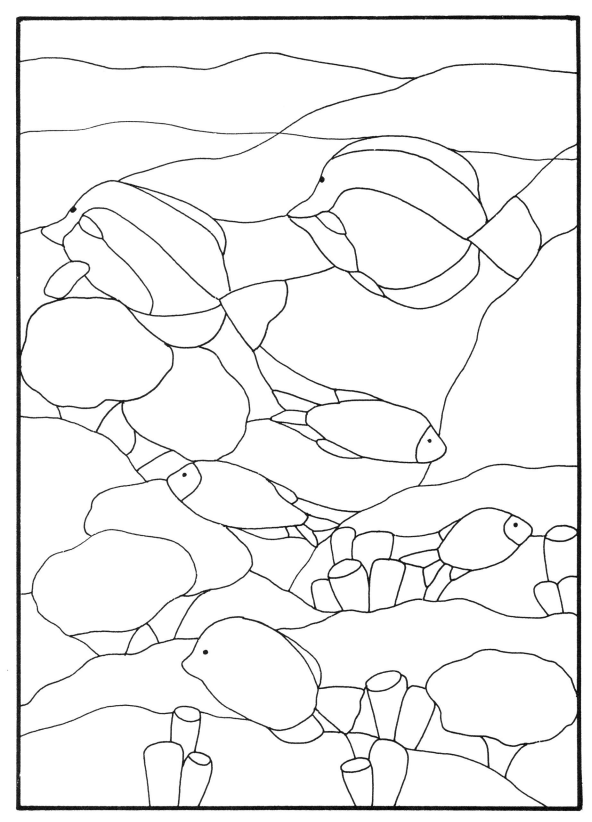

Underwater Scene

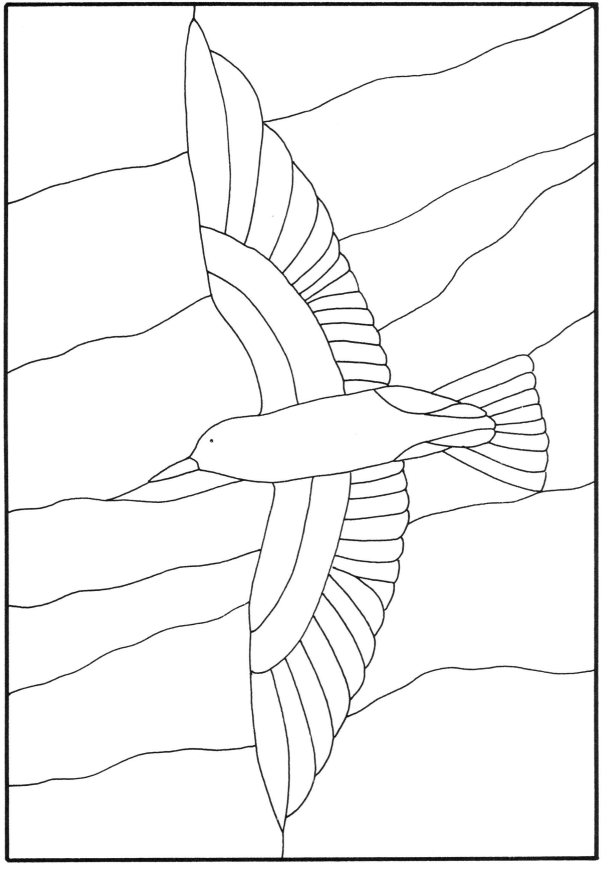

Gull

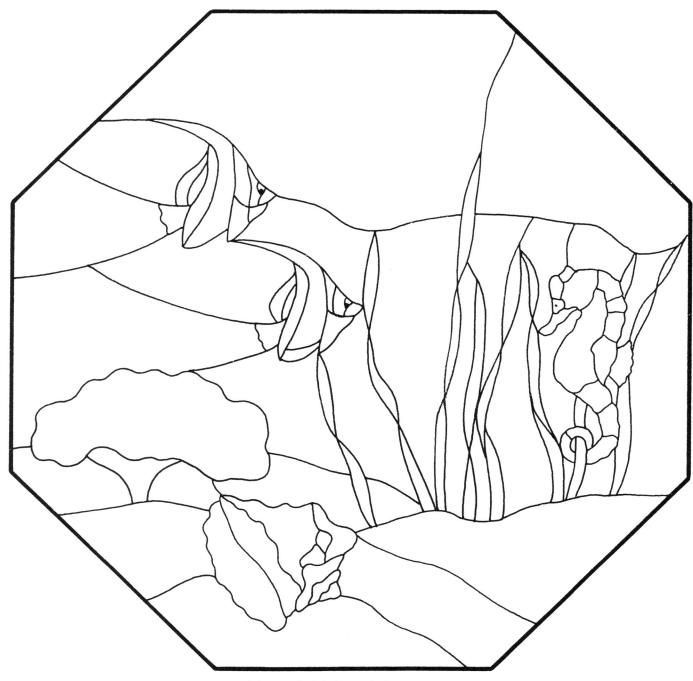

Moorish Idols and Sea Horse

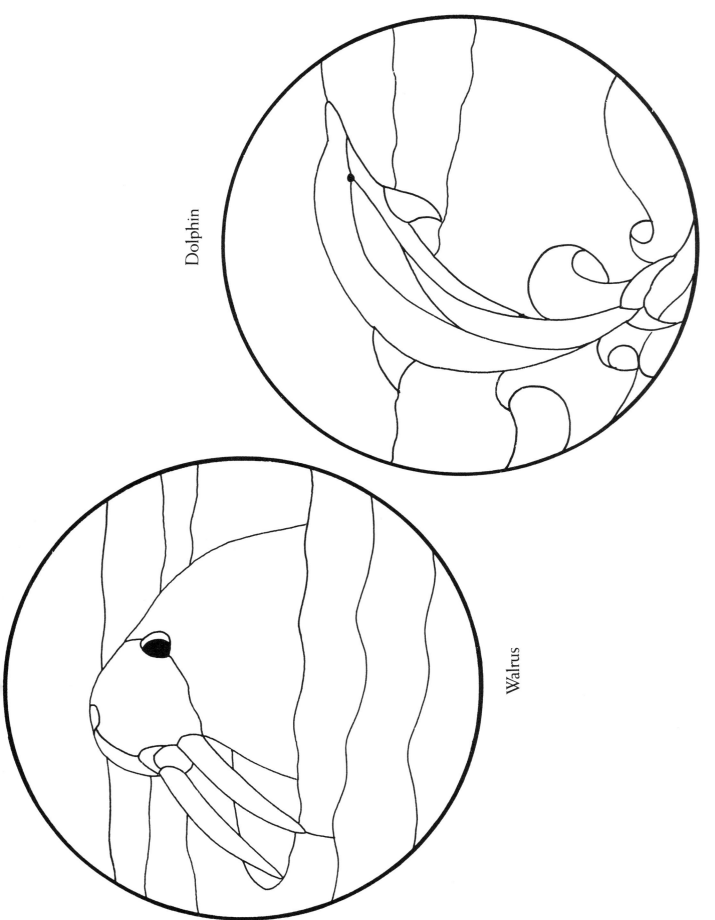

Dolphin

Walrus

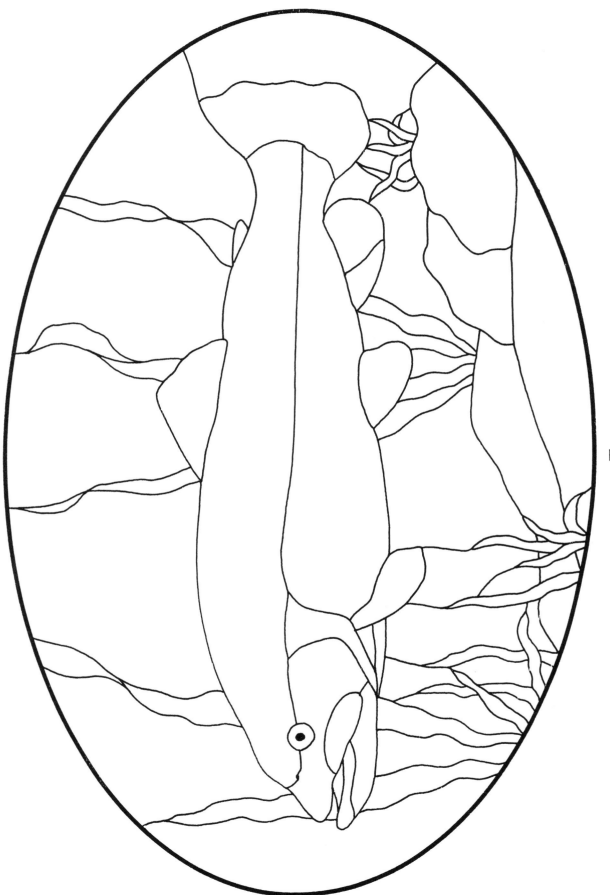

Trout

Grouper

Trigger Fish

Jellyfish

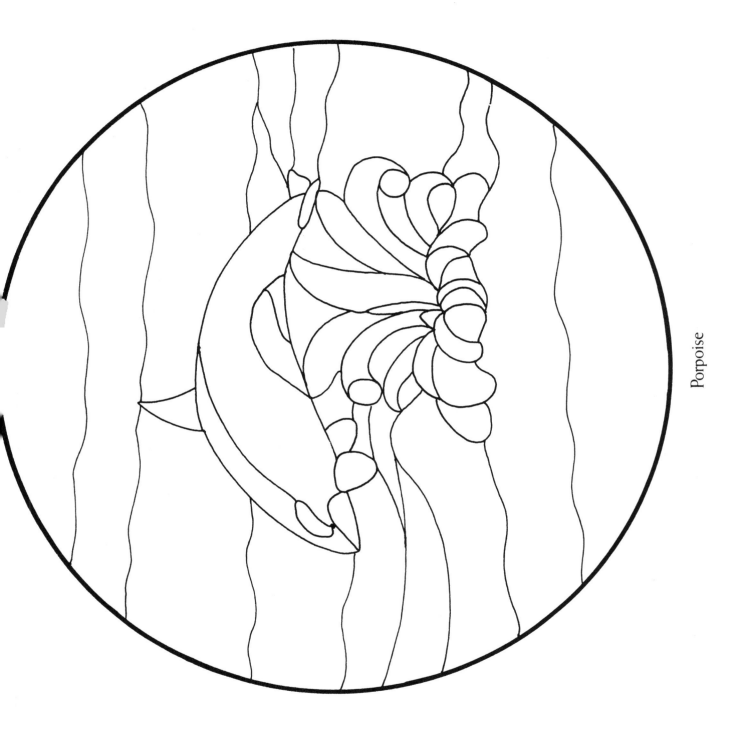

Porpoise

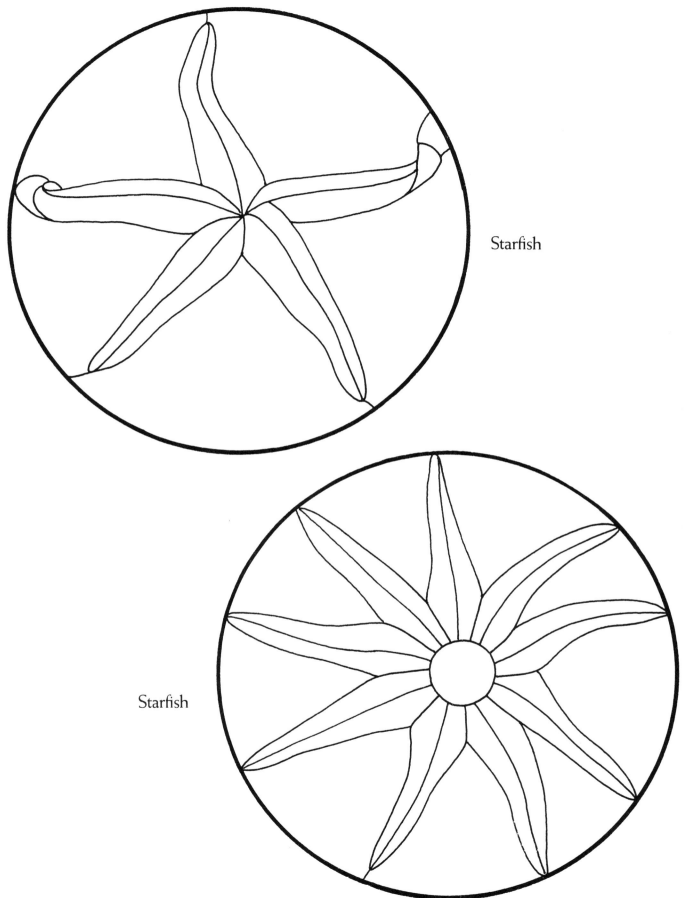

Starfish

Starfish

Octopus

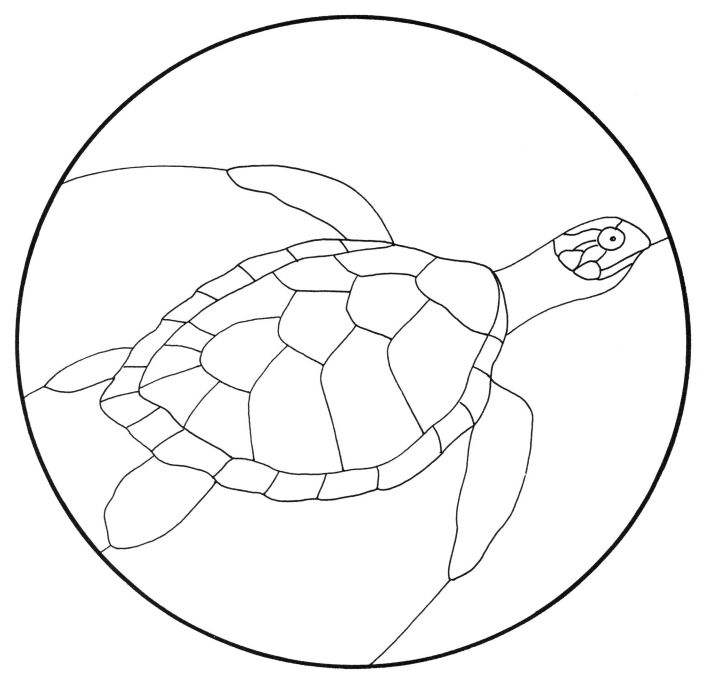

Sea Turtle

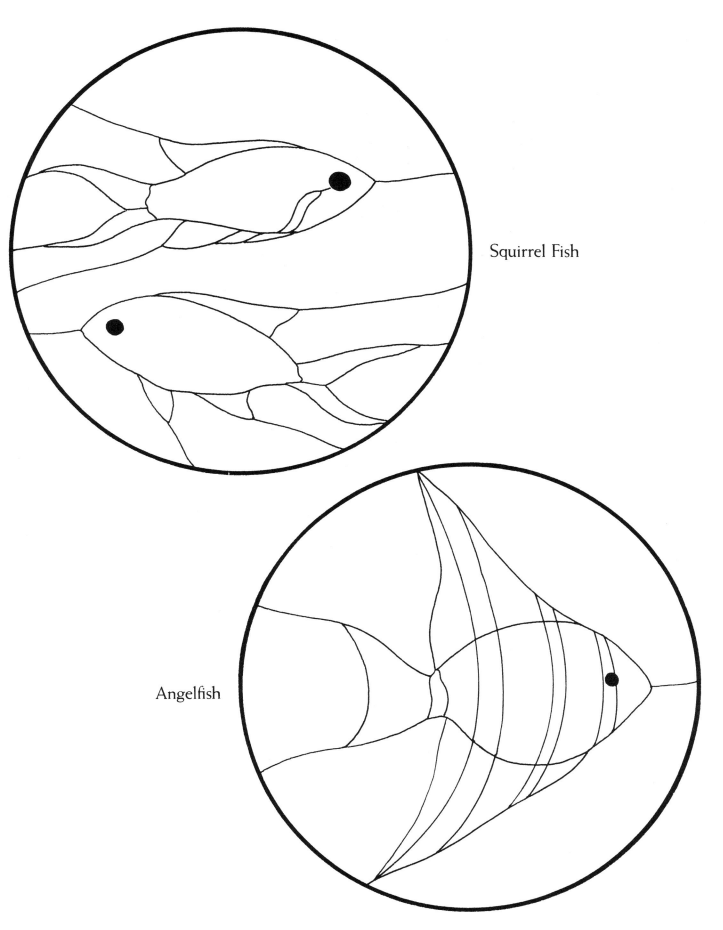

Squirrel Fish

Angelfish

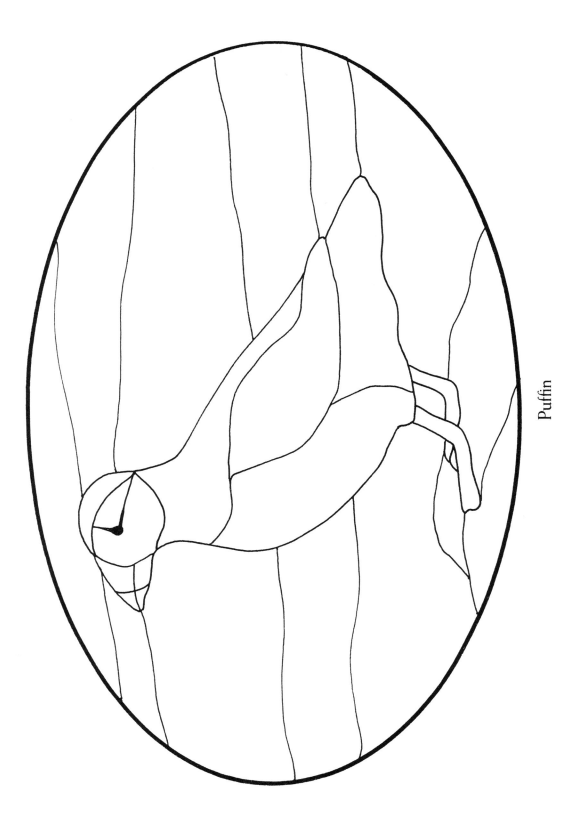

Puffin

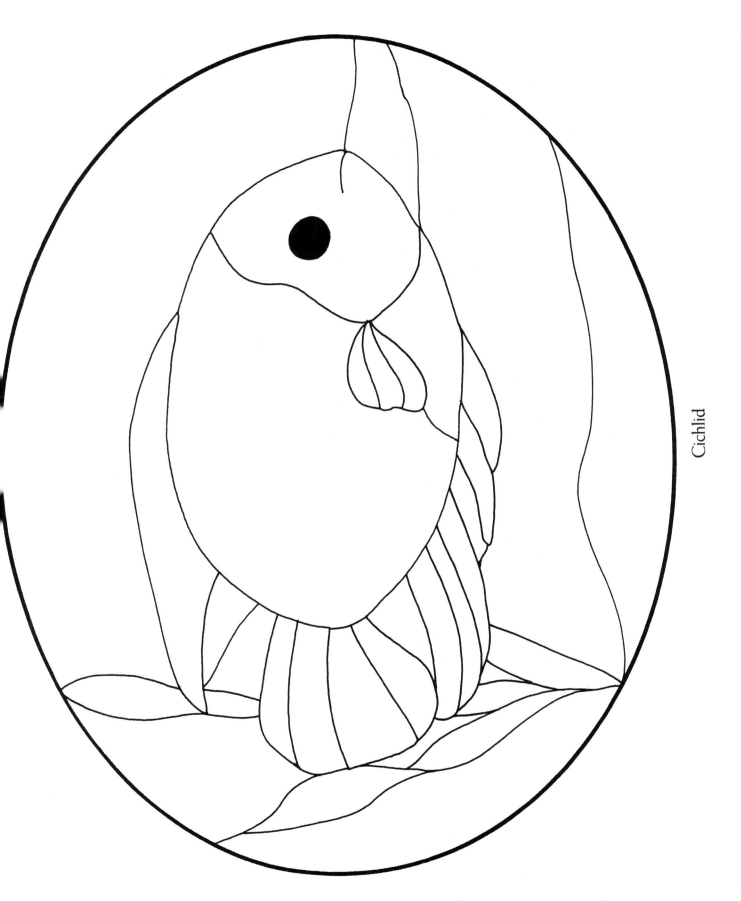

Cichlid

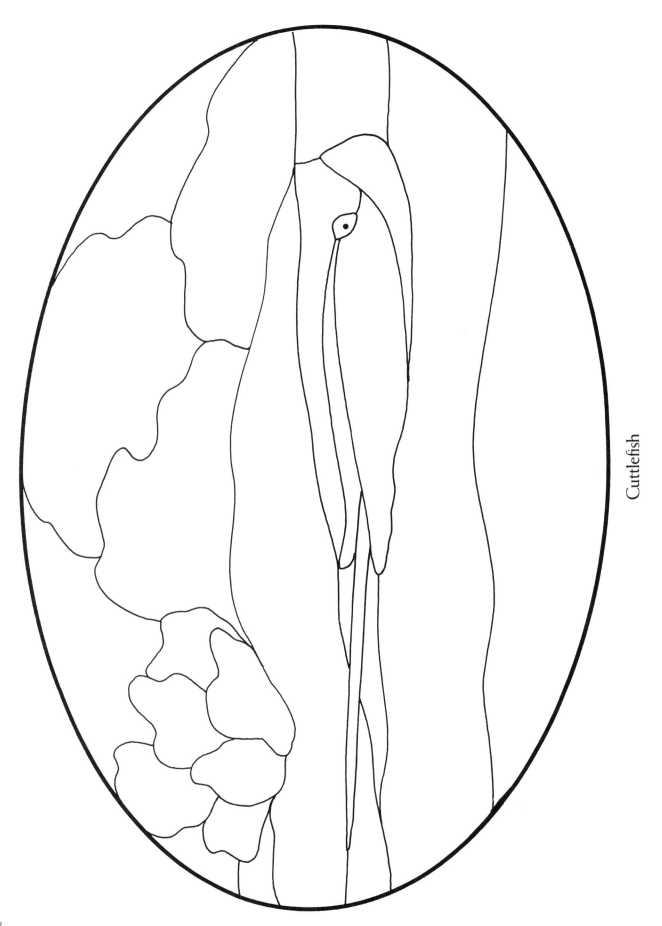

Cuttlefish

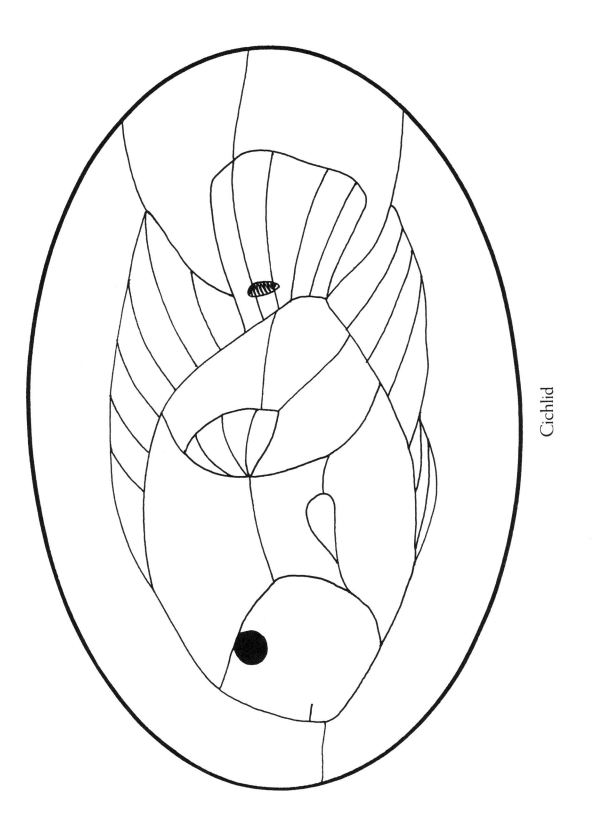

Cichlid

Squid and Snails

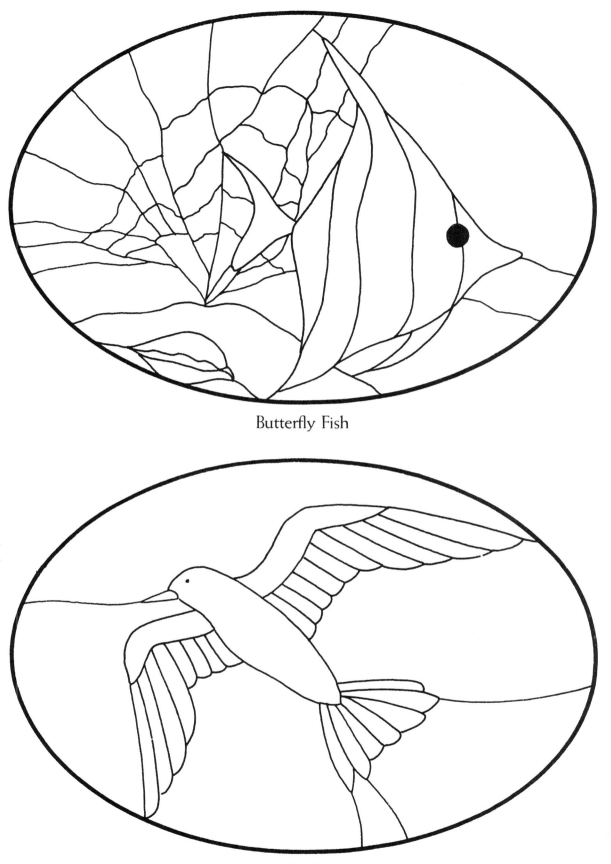

Butterfly Fish

Gull

Parrot Fish

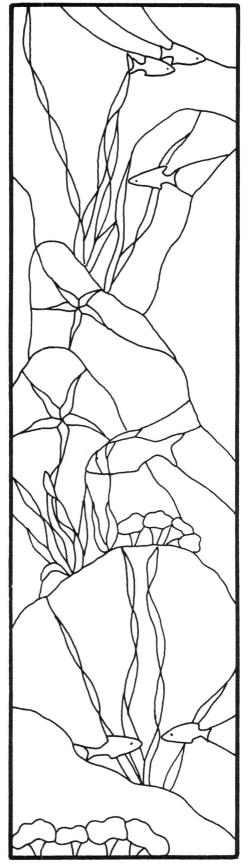

Underwater Scene

Underwater Scene

Clownfish

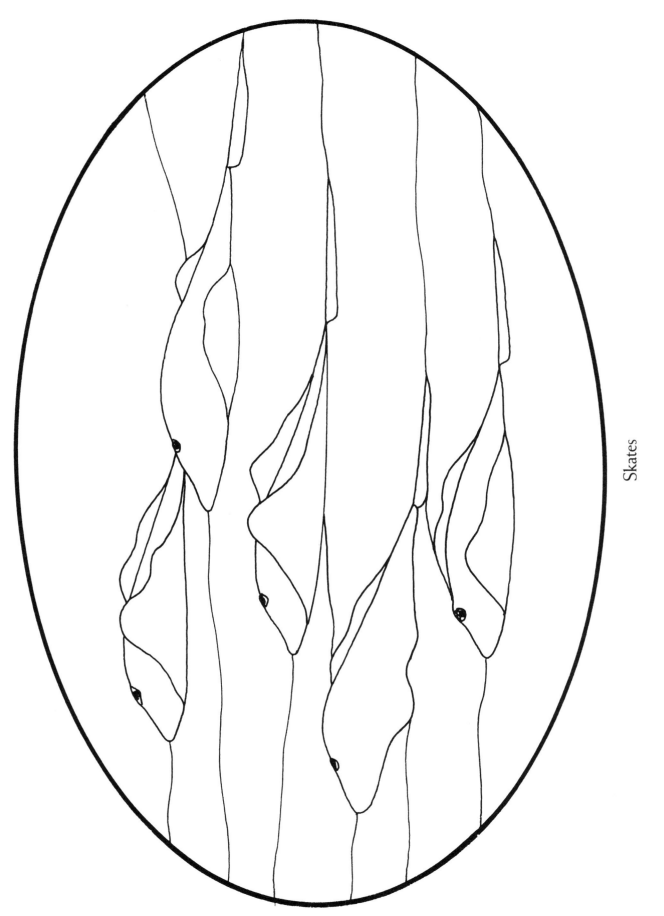

Skates

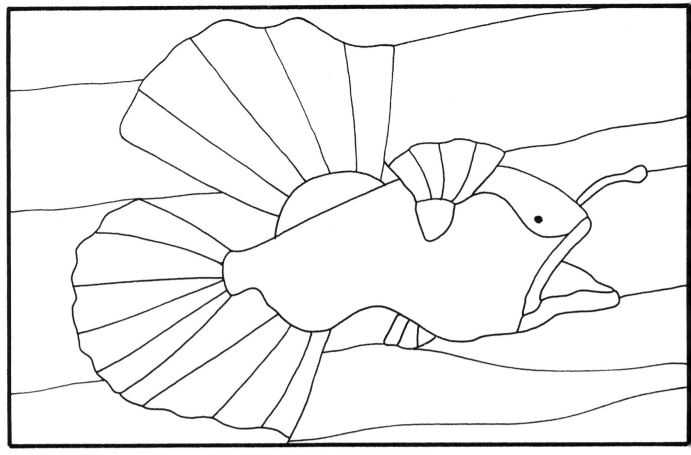

Anglerfish

Herring

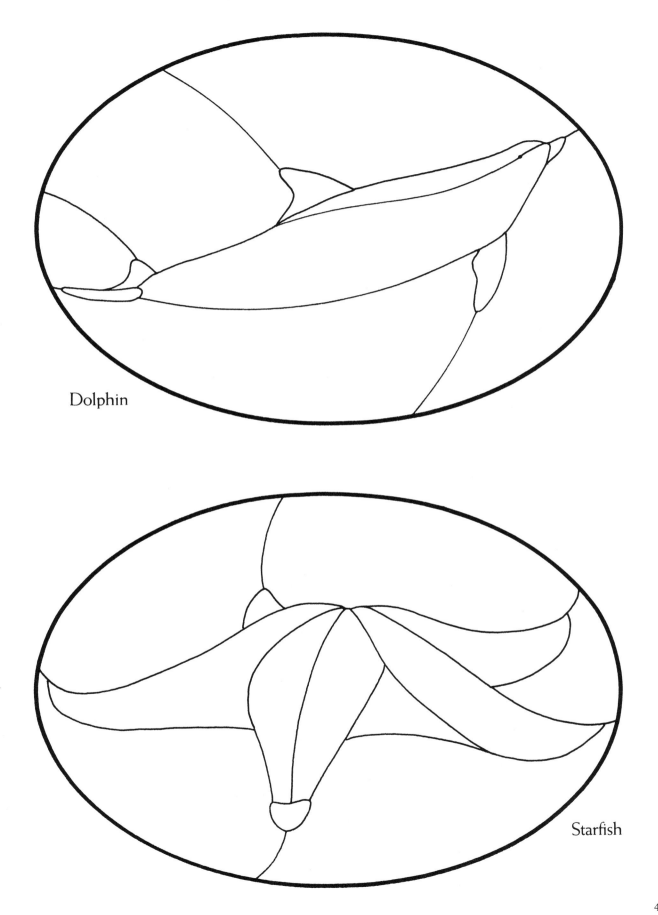

Dolphin

Starfish

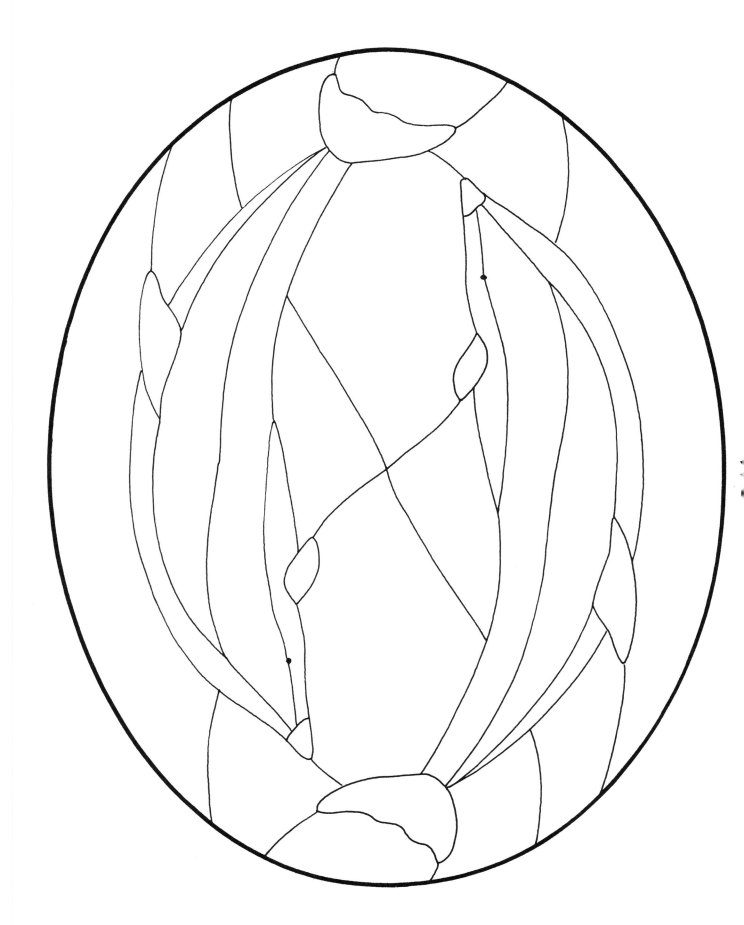

Damselfish

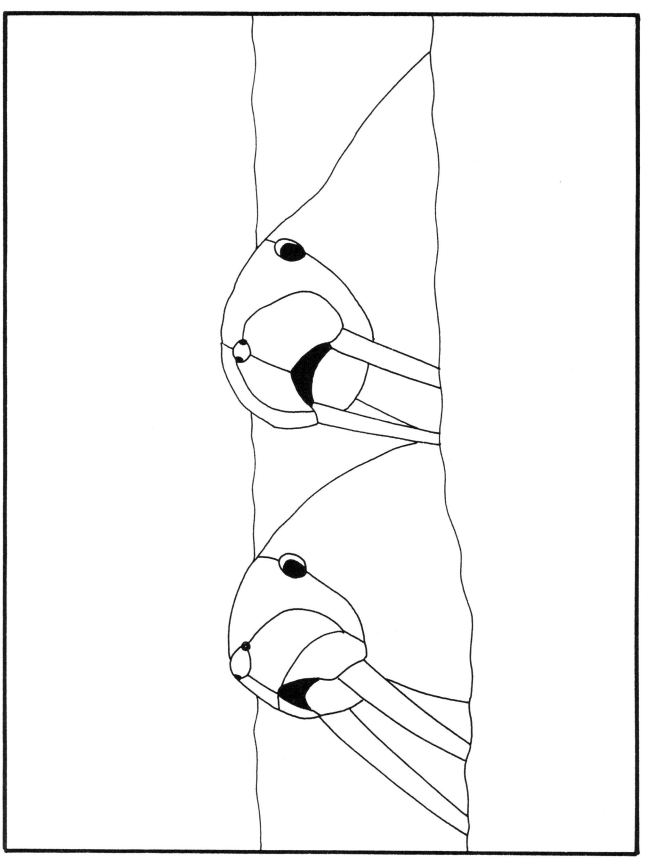

Walruses

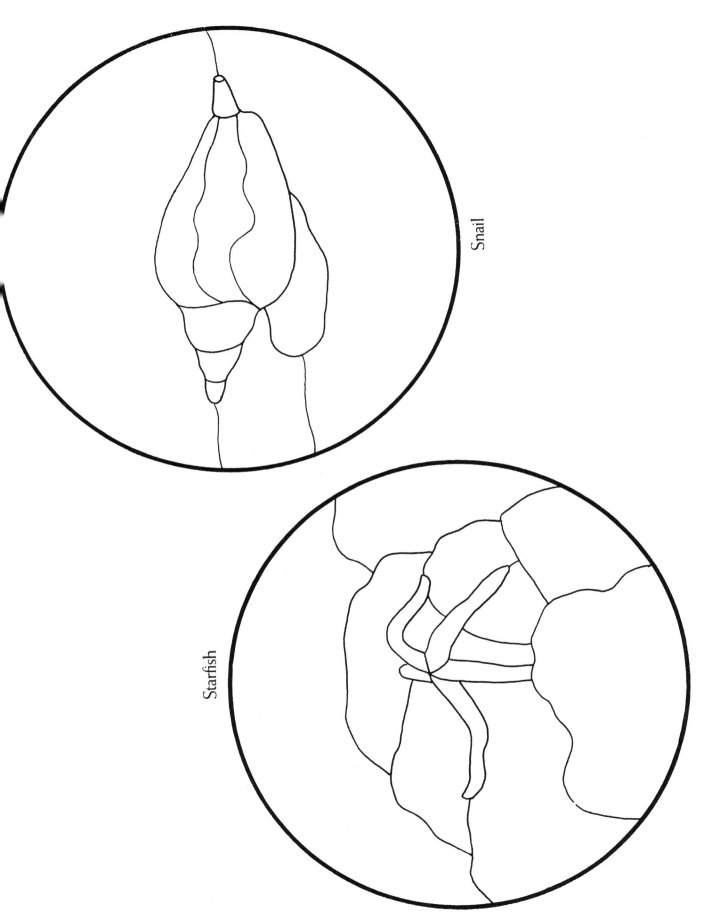

Snail

Starfish

51

Bass

Underwater Scene

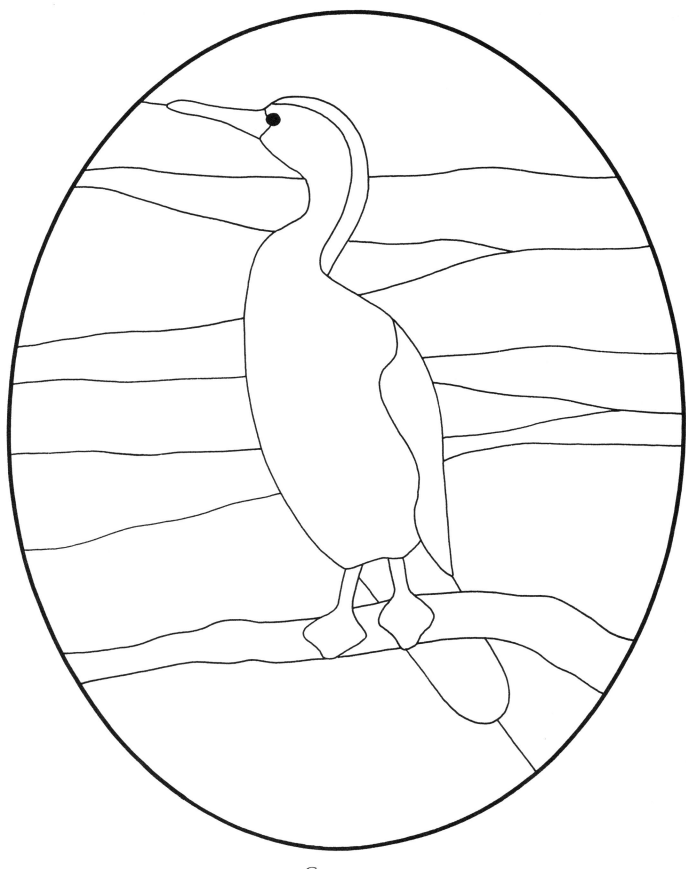

Cormorant

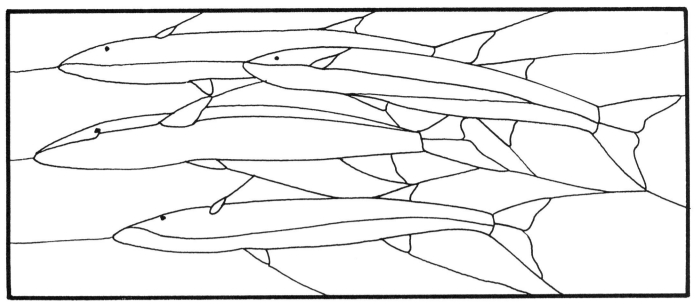

Mackerel

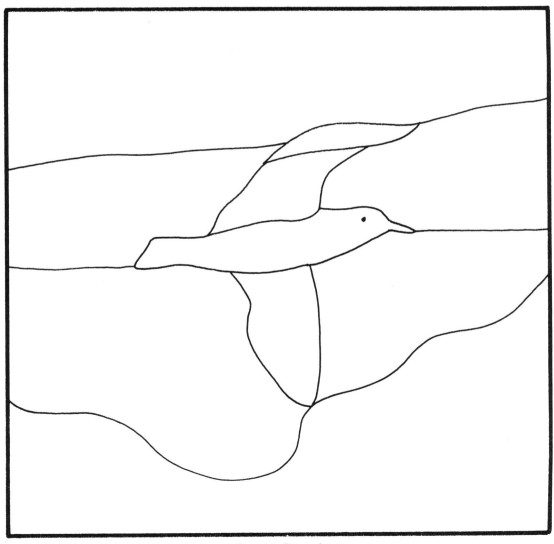

Storm Petrel

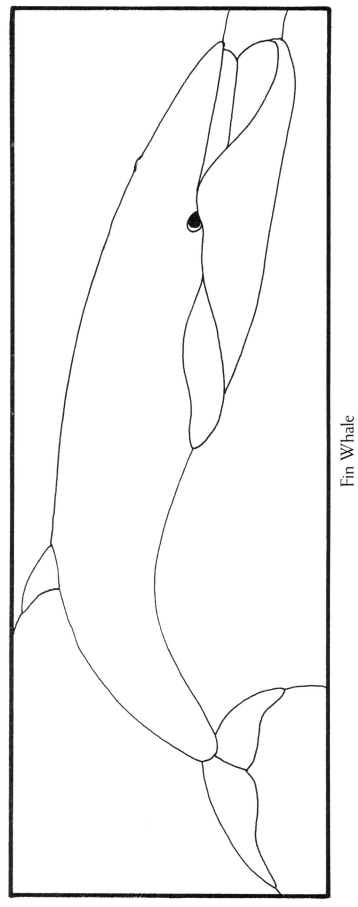

Fin Whale

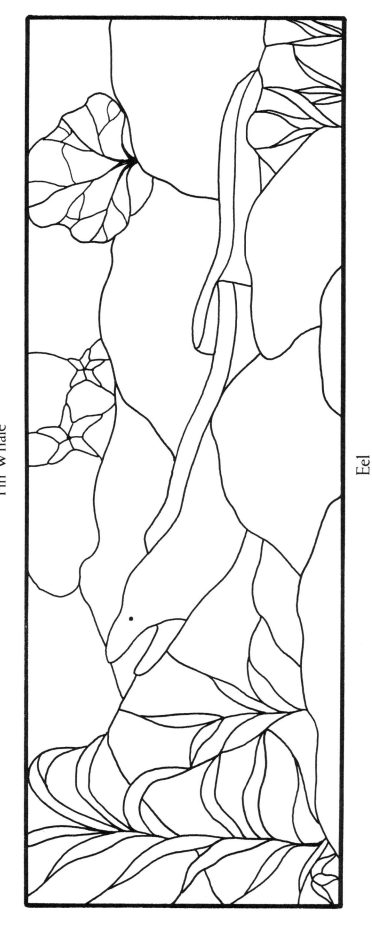

Eel

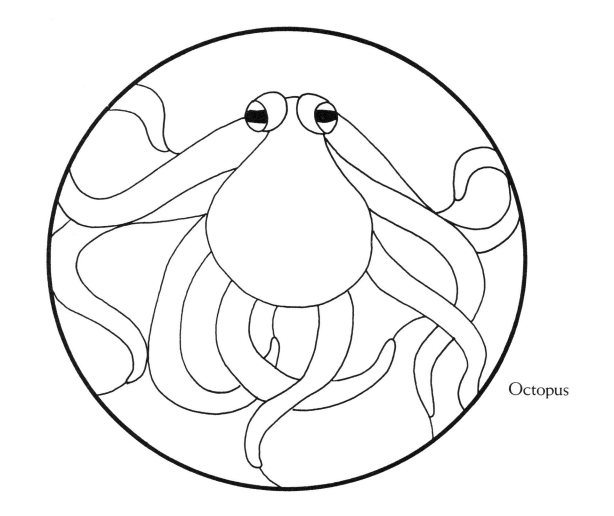

Octopus

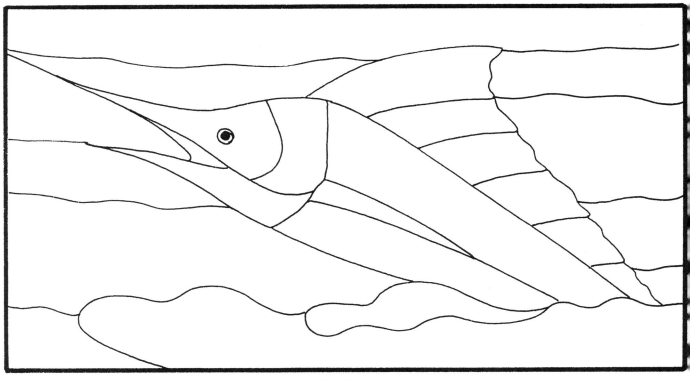

Sailfish

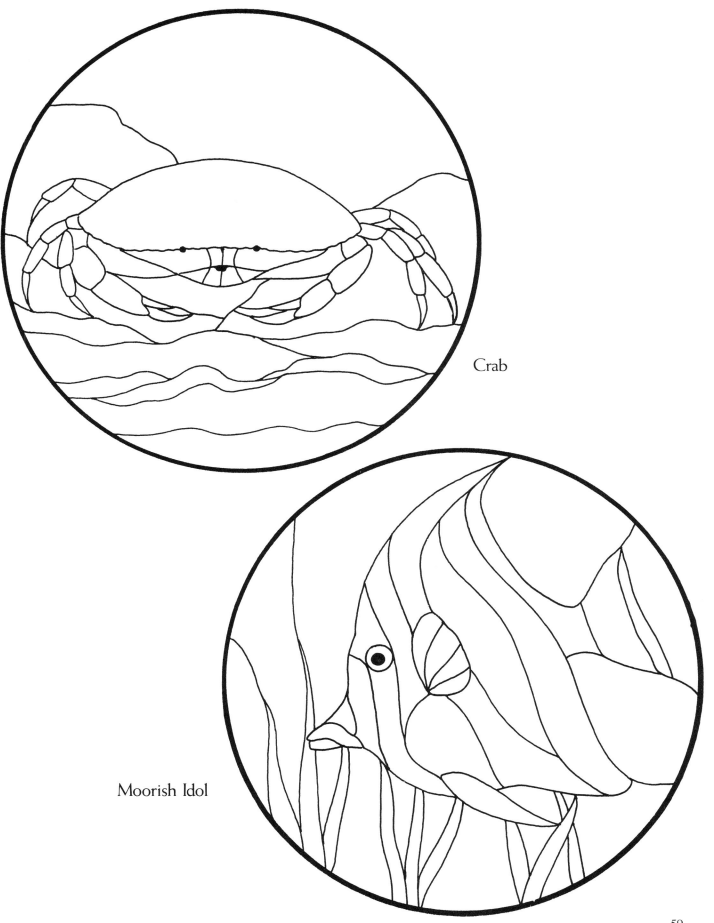

Crab

Moorish Idol

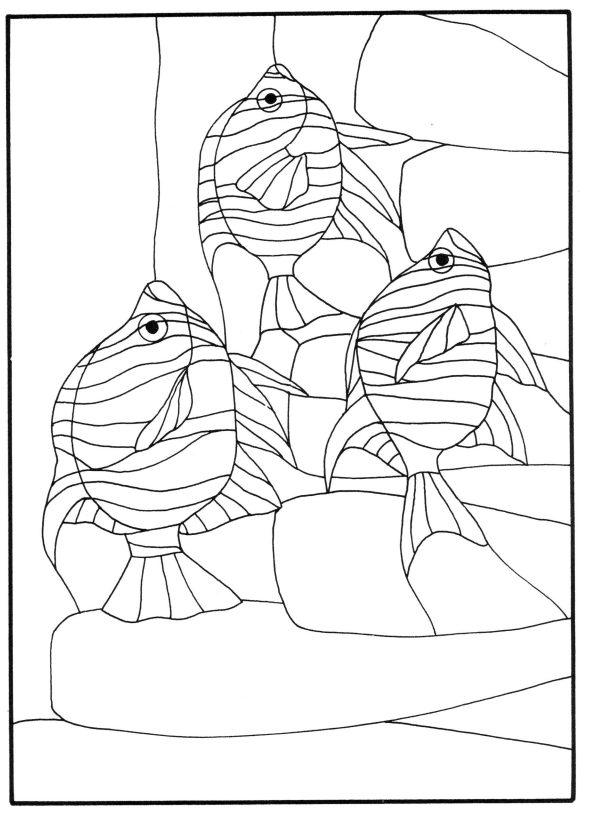

Butterfly Fish